URBAN SKETCHING
DISAPPEARING LANDMARKS IN
TORONTO

RECORDING TORONTO'S ENDANGERED LANDMARKS ONE DRAWING AT A TIME

TORONTO URBAN SKETCHERS
www.torontourbansketchers.blogspot.ca

Urban Sketching Disappearing Landmarks in Toronto.
Copyright (c) 2015 by the Toronto Urban Sketchers

ISBN-13: 978-1519643247
ISBN-10: 1519643241

Image Credits
Front cover : McLaughlin Planetarium by Marion Younan
Back cover : Guildwood Inn Park and Garden by Beibei Yu

Research : Barry Stoch
Writing : Helen Wilkie and Marie-Judith Jean-Louis
Editing : Denise Job
Layout and design : Marie-Judith Jean-Louis

URBAN SKETCHING
DISAPPEARING LANDMARKS IN
TORONTO

TORONTO URBAN SKETCHERS
www.torontourbansketchers.blogspot.ca

CONTENTS

INTRODUCTION	7
OUR MANIFESTO	9
HONEST ED'S	11
O'CONNOR BOWL	20
ST-LAWRENCE MARKET NORTH	20
LOBLAW WAREHOUSE	21
CAPTAIN JOHN'S BOAT RESTAURANT	23
MUSEUM OF CONTEMPORARY CANADIAN ART	29
60 MILLS	29
MCLAUGHLIN	31
PLANETARIUM	31
GUILDWOOD INN PARK AND GARDEN	39
RICHARD L. HEARN GENERATING STATION	46
WILLIAM DINEEN HOUSE	49
CANADA BREAD	51
BIG BEE SHOP	51
PARADISE THEATRE	51
HERITAGE BUILDINGS ON CHURCH ST.	53
DE LASALLE COLLEGE	61
DEER PARK UNITED CHURCH	61
THE COOKBOOK	63
STORE	63

(left to right, top to bottom):

1) Farid Ahmadi 2) Perry Chow 3) Nicole Contois 4) Patricia DeSilva 5) David Edwards 6) Barbara Eguchi 7) Marie-Judith Jean-Louis 8) Denise Job 9) Henry Lo 10) Nora MacPhail 11) Mauricio Munoz 12) Hasibush Shaheed 13) Li Shen 14) Barry Stoch 15) Amara Strand 16) Adina Vomisescu 17) Helen Wilkie 18) Marion Younan 19) Beibei Yu

Meet the **TORONTO URBAN SKETCHERS** featured in this book

INTRODUCTION

During the summer of 2015, a group of urban sketchers from Toronto set out to sketch some of the disappearing landmarks in the city of Toronto. As the city keeps growing and new buildings get erected, some of the landmarks are taking a back seat and slowly disappearing and fading in the background. This project was a way to tell the story of these landmarks from different points of views and connect with some of the history of the city. We also hope to raise awareness of the effects of the disappearance of older buildings and structures, express the beauty we see in the old, the historical, the disappearing traces of the city's past.

The Toronto Urban Sketchers group was created 2 years prior as a way to bring like-minded creatives together to tell the stories of their city and the places they travel to, one sketch at a time. The mission of urban sketchers is to raise the artistic, storytelling and educational value of location drawing, promote its practice and connect people around the world who draw on location where they live and travel. We aim to show the world, one drawing at a time.

For more info about the Toronto Urban Sketchers visit http://toronto-urbansketchers.blogspot.ca/

Photo by Marie-Judith Jean-Louis

OUR MANIFESTO

Photo by Oliver Tsuji

We draw on location, indoors or out,
capturing what we see from direct observation.

Our drawings tell the story of our surroundings,
the places we live and where we travel.

Our drawings are a record of time and place.

We are truthful to the scenes we witness.

We use any kind of media and cherish our
individual styles.

We support each other and draw together.

We share our drawings online.

We show the world, one drawing at a time

http://toronto-urbansketchers.blogspot.ca/

Hashibush Shaheed

HONEST ED'S

Honest Ed's is one of those places that can't really be understood any other way than by visiting it. Stand outside and admire the brightly coloured and lighted signage, and you might be forgiven for thinking it's not a store but a carnival attraction. But yes, it is a store.

Honest Ed was a real person. Ed Mirvish was a European immigrant who achieved great success in Canada through hard work and innovation. He opened Honest Ed's BargainHouse in 1948, and its popularity soon led to an expansion. It now runs a whole city block on the corner of Bloor and Bathurst Streets.

Many store signs are lit up — but not many with 23,000 light bulbs! The big red and yellow frontage is also famous for its cheesy slogans, such as "Welcome, don't faint at our low prices, there's no place to lie down!"

Ed Mirvish was known as much for his generosity as for his skill as a merchant. His longstanding tradition of giving away free turkeys at Christmas and Thanksgiving has been continued by his son, David Mirvish.

In October 2013, the property was sold to Westbank Properties, a Vancouver-based developer of luxury hotels and residences. At that time, David Mirvish announced he would rent the property from Westbank until the developer decided what to do with the land, during which time the store will continue to operate.

When its time runs out at the end of 2016, the demise of Honest Ed's will mark the end of a unique Toronto icon.

Amara Strand

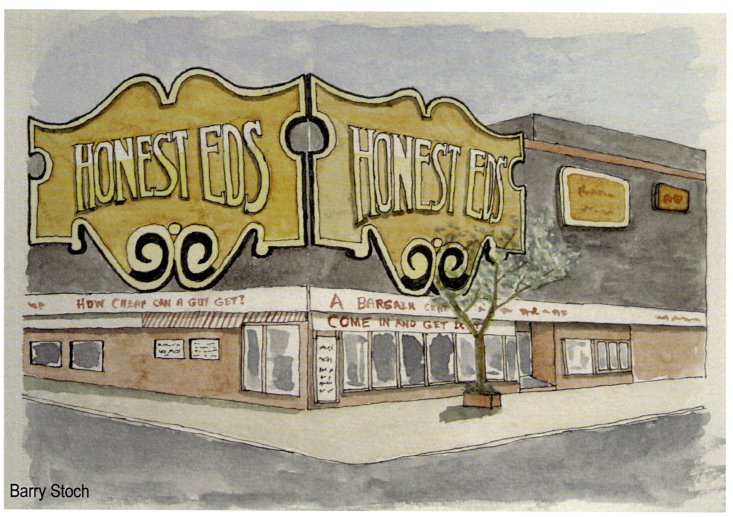

Barry Stoch

Perry Chow

Adina Vomisescu

Hashibush Shaheed

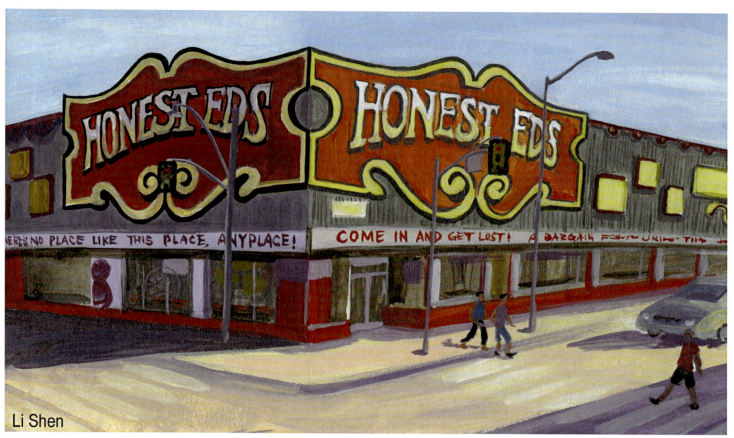

Li Shen

Mauricio Munoz

Patricia DeSilva

Marie-Judith Jean-Louis

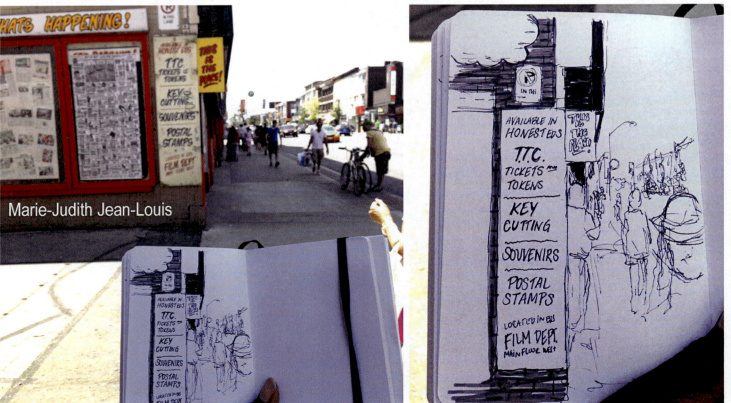

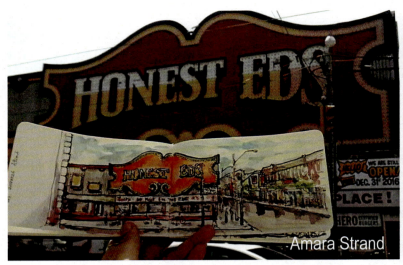
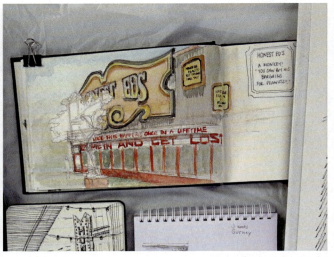

Amara Strand

Marie-Judith Jean-Louis

David Edwards

Ken Yuen

O'CONNOR BOWL

O'Connor Bowl closed earlier this year to be replaced by another condominium project. It is said to have been one of the few remaining old school bowling alleys in Toronto and used to be a great gathering place in the past for parties and televised sporting events.

Barry Stoch

Barbara Eguchi

ST-LAWRENCE MARKET NORTH

Amara Strand

LOBLAW WAREHOUSE

Mauricio Munoz

Ken Yuen

Beibei Yu

Nora MacPhail

CAPTAIN JOHN'S BOAT RESTAURANT

Captain John's, located for most of its existence in a former Adriatic passenger ship called the MS Jadran, was a familiar sight to Torontonians and visitors alike. It was permanently docked at the foot of Yonge Street at 1 Queen's Quay West for almost forty years.

Once a prestige destination, the well known seafood restaurant was open every day of the year, including all major holidays.

The ship caught people's imagination immediately, possibly because at the time it opened the waterfront was an industrial portland. The redevelopment of the Harbourfront turned the area into a recreational destination for both residents and tourists, as well as an upscale residential neighbourhood.

In 2002, however, there began a long period of difficulties for Captain John's, including personal financial and family difficulties for the owner, John Letnik. Matters grew worse, and in 2008 the restaurant ran afoul of the Toronto Public Health Department, which cited numerous infractions of health regulations.

After several unsuccessful attempts to find a buyer for the ship, in May 2015 the Federal Court approved plans to have it towed to the Marine Recycling Corporation's facility at Port Colborne, Ontario, to be scrapped. On May 28, 2015 the old ship was towed out of the harbour to begin its final voyage, witnessed by a crowd of several hundred people and an impromptu band.

Its empty berth now stands silent witness to the end of an era.

Barry Stoch

Farid Ahmadi

Helen Wilkie

Farid Ahmadi

Barbara Eguchi

Photo by Marie-Judith Jean-Louis

Farid Ahmadi

Nora MacPhail

Hasibush Shaheed

Amara Strand

Photo by Marie-Judith Jean-Louis

Marie-Judith Jean-Louis

MUSEUM OF CONTEMPORARY CANADIAN ART

The Museum of Contemporary Canadian Art found a new home. As such, the repurposed warehouse located in Queen West that used to be its home for the past 10 years will be redeveloped in the near future. The plans are to demolish the building to make way for a new condominium development.

Patricia DeSilva

60 MILLS

Amara Strand

David Edwards

MCLAUGHLIN PLANETARIUM

The McLaughlin Planetarium, 100 Queen's Park Circle
The McLaughlin Planetarium generated a great deal of excitement when it opened to the public on October 26, 1968. Nothing like it had ever been seen in Toronto, and indeed its state-of-the-art electro-mechanical Zeiss planetarium projector made the wonders of the heavens accessible to visitors of all ages.

In the seventies, major construction at the Royal Ontario Museum, the planetarium's sibling next door, led to a decline in attendance for the planetarium as well as the demolition of some of its facilities.

In the 1980s, the planetarium's sound system and domed ceiling became the stars of the show, as dazzling music-themed laser light shows delighted audiences reclining in the wonderfully comfortable seats.

For those whose interests lay in the stars themselves and the vast space around them, the planetarium's lower levels featured the Astrocentre, a gallery that related the history of astronomy through artifacts and exhibits. It also housed the world's first Stellarium, a three-dimensional map of the stars.

Although the number of visitors to the planetarium picked up when the museum reopened in 1984, sadly it closed on November 5, 1995 due to provincial budget cuts to the museum. Its exhibits, artifacts and theatre facilities were dismantled and dispersed.

The planetarium's star shone briefly again when it housed The Children's Own Museum, but it is now used by the ROM mainly for storage and offices.

The planetarium was founded in 1968 by a grant from philanthropist Colonel R. Samuel McLaughlin, and after its varied 46-year history the ROM sold both the site and the building to the University of Toronto. The University plans to demolish the building to make way for new facilities.

Amara Strand

Helen Wilkie

Marie-Judith Jean-Louis

Patricia DeSilva

Photo by Marie-Judith Jean-Louis

Patricia DeSilva

David Edwards

Photo by Marie-Judith Jean-Louis

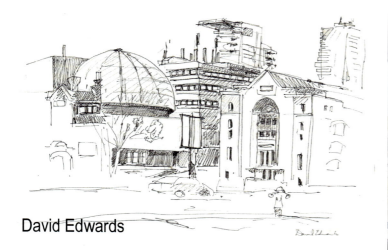

David Edwards

Nicole Contois

Hasibush Shaheed

Marion Younan

Hasibush Shaheed

McLaughlin Planetarium
June 6, 2015
-back entrance-

Denise Job

Photo by Marie-Judith Jean-Louis

Barbara Eguchi

GUILDWOOD INN PARK AND GARDEN

It was recently announced that after decades of negotiations, the Guild Inn will be revitalized. The Hotel has been closed since 2001 and fell off the radar of many Torontonians.

This was once the estate of Colonel Harold C. Bickford. A concrete hotel that was part of this estate had been demolished in 2009 and it seems like the future of the site was uncertain until it was taken over by Dynamic Hospitality and Entertainment Group Inc who plan to restore the site and reopen it in 2016. While demolition work is expected for some of the more damaged structures, most are hopeful that the essence of the site will remain. Only time will tell.

Such a lovely day! I did this sketch today at Guild Park.

This place, which has many architectural buildings, is worth visiting.
In 1999, the park was designated a heritage property by the Heritage Canada Foundation. The building was a historic hotel and Depression-era artist colony. It was proposed to be torn down for a redevelopment of the area.
Guild Park is a sculpture garden consisting of the rescued facades and ruins. The hotel was closed by 2001.

In front of this building, there are architectural fragments and sculptures in the gardens. We sat under the shade and sketched this abandoned building. Some neighbours came to the parks and a dog ran to us, seems she was also interested in what we were sketching. The fence was built around the building, but I skipped it.

- Perry Chow

Another day I came again to sketch another side of the inn. There is so much to draw - such as the beautiful garden, the sculptures and the view of Lake Ontario. When I walked around to find a spot to sketch, I found that the soil was all wet. It didn't rain. I was wondering if this was because Lake Ontario is right in front of the gardens.

- Perry Chow

Perry Chow

Li Shen

Barbara Eguchi

Barry Stoch

Beibei Yu

Liz Creswick

LI SHEN
2015.7

Li Shen

Nora MacPhail

RICHARD L. HEARN GENERATING STATION

The Richard L. Hearn Generating Station is a electrical generating station, that has been decommissioned since 1983 and has been standing abandoned for years.

There had been talks about demolishing the station in the past but it seems to have caught the interest of the organizers of the Luminato Festival with talks about transforming the power plant into a public art centre for the festival's 10th anniversary in 2016 with the hopes of turning it into "the world's largest multidisciplinary generator of art and culture".

Mauricio Munoz

Perry Chow

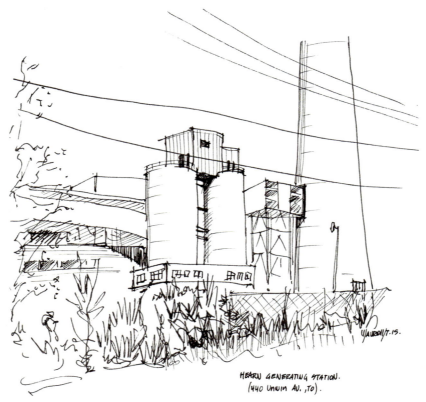

Mauricio Munoz

Barry Stoch

Li Shen

WILLIAM DINEEN HOUSE

William Dineen House, 230 Sherbourne Street

William Dineen, a successful Toronto businessman and community leader in the late 19th century, was co-founder of the W. and D. Dineen Company, Furriers and Clothiers. For nearly forty years, he lived in the beautiful old house located at 230 Sherbourne Street.

In marked contrast to the present time, this area was an upscale residential neighbourhood in the late 19th centure. Not surprisingly, updating and alterations to the original building in 1895 were undertaken by the prestigious architectural firm of Langley and Langley.

The style of the house is typical of upscale residences of its time. Its lovely terra cotta finish has kept its vivid brightness, providing a bold splash of colour in its current surroundings.

Although Dineen House has been designated a Heritage Building, its future seems still to be in doubt. The present owner submitted a demotion application, which was subsequently withdrawn. The vacant lot next door, however, was formerly home to a similar building which was in fact torn down.

David Edwards

CANADA BREAD

That was my old neighbourhood before I moved to Parkdale in late 1986! I even remembered that there was a bowling alley in that spot before it burned down in 1978 (I saw it from my aunt's balcony and I was only 11 then)!

Nicole Contois

BIG BEE SHOP

" *While waiting for my son's appointment at St Clair Clinic on the south-west corner I witnessed the destruction and reconstruction of the South-East corner of Bathurst/St Clair St. intersection. There was this little Big Bee Shop that I often ordered my coffee and a juice for my son. Now it is gone.*"

Adina Vomisescu

PARADISE THEATRE

Beibei Yu

Amara Strand

HERITAGE BUILDINGS ON CHURCH ST.

Heritage buildings in the Gay Village, 580-596 Church and 65, 67, 69 Gloucester St

Toronto has been called a city of neighbourhoods. These small enclaves tend to have a strong sense of their own identity within the larger city. Toronto's Gay Village on Church Street is no exception.

Besides its vibrant gay community, the area is known for a number of heritage buildings on Church and Gloucester Streets. These beautiful old houses survived threat of demolition by a developer planning a condo building in 2011, largely due to the community's outspoken opposition.

A fine example of the Second Empire architectural style, 580-582 Church Street dates back to 1878. At 584 Church Street stands the Catherine Collard House, a 3-story detached home built in 1909. The Wallace Millichamp House, located at 592 Church Street, has served as a rental apartment building for many years. At the corner of Church and Gloucester Streets is a 3-story apartment building built in 1911.

All of these individual parts of Toronto's history would have been partially or completely destroyed by the proposed condo building. Although residents of the Village today can celebrate their victory in preventing the development, constant vigilance seems to be indicated.

David Edwards

Helen Wilkie

Amara Strand

Amara Strand

Photo by Marie-Judith Jean-Louis

Diana Tsigg

Li Shen

Denise Job

Li Shen

Amara Strand

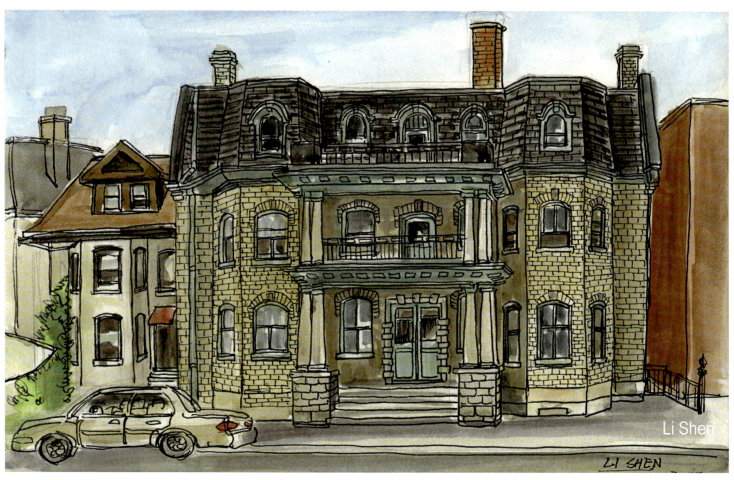

Li Shen

Henry Lo

Hasibush Shaheed

Marie-Judith Jean-Louis

Farid Ahmadi

Farid Ahmadi

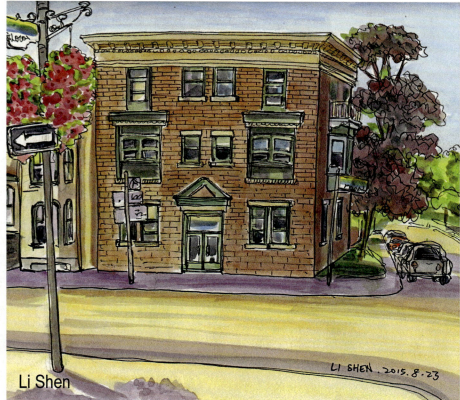

Li Shen

Amara Strand

Patricia DeSilva

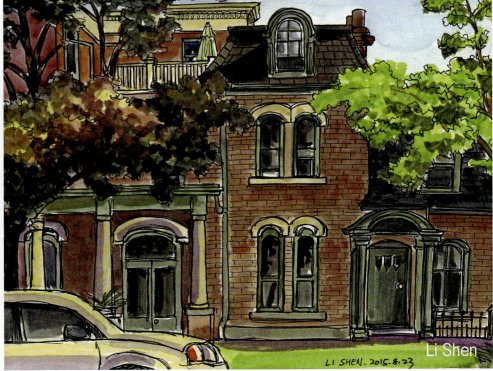
Li Shen

DEER PARK UNITED CHURCH

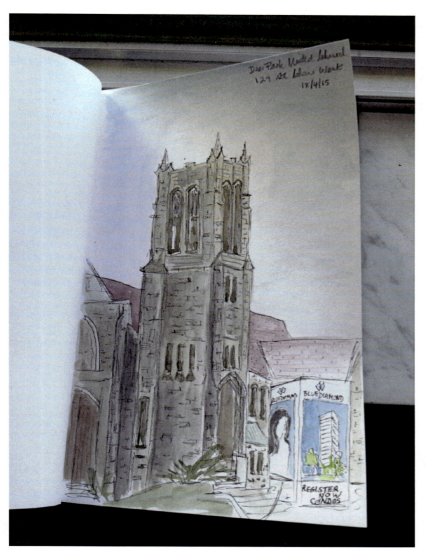

Deer Park United Church, St. Clair and Avenue Road. I belong to this congregation and although we are now happily ensconced in another building, it was sad to leave this one. I see from the billboard that they are now registering condos, so I guess it won't be long before this lovely old church becomes part of a condo project.

Helen Wilkie

THE FIELDHOUSE DE LA SALLE COLLEGE

Marion Younan

Patricia DeSilva

THE COOKBOOK STORE

What do Julia Child, Anthony Bourdain and Nigella Lawson have in common? Why, they've all been guest presenters at Toronto's iconic Cookbook Store!

There's a lot of talk today about niche marketing, but back in 1983 it wasn't so well known. So Dr. Josh Josephson was a retail pioneer when he jumped into a narrow niche and opened The Cookbook Store in the old Frogley Building at the corner of Yonge and Yorkville.

Lovers of cooking — or just cook books — found their bliss poring over the blend of beautifully produced books that showed cooking as an art form and the simply practical recipes people were more likely to actually make. It was a destination store, as well as a drop-in find, for many cooking enthusiasts over its 31 years.

The Frogley Building's food connection doesn't start with The Cookbook Store, however, as Charles J. Frogley bought the building in 1885 and operated a confectionery store and bakery. There is even an unconfirmed rumor that George Weston learned to bake bread when he worked at Frogley's as a lad of twelve!

But Toronto's seemingly voracious appetite for condo development caught up with The Cookbook Store, and it closed in March 2014 to make way for the 58-story 1 Yorkville Tower.

When a group of Urban Sketchers arrived to sketch on August 8, 2015, they found the store already closed, its sign gone and its formerly colourful windows covered over with brown paper. Undeterred, they recorded it anyway, but it is fortunate that individual members had made their sketches earlier, while it still held a suggestion of its former glory.

Diana Tsigg

Diana Tsigg

Henry Lo

Amara Strand

Hasibush Shaheed

Hasibush Shaheed

Photo by Marie-Judith Jean-Louis

Marie-Judith Jean-Louis

Helen Wilkie

The Toronto Urban Sketchers is a group of art enthusiasts from various backgrounds who meet regularly around the city and illustrate it from their unique perspective. The group is a chapter of the international urban sketchers whose mission is to raise the artistic storytelling and educational value of location drawing, promoting its practice and connecting people around the world who draw on location where they live and travel.

The Toronto chapter was founded by Marie-Judith Jean-Louis in 2013, as a way to meet and connect with like-minded people to explore the city.

Made in the USA
Middletown, DE
14 February 2016